A Note From Rick Renner

I am on a personal quest to see a "revival of the Bible" so people can establish their lives on a firm foundation that will stand strong and endure the test as end-time storm winds begin to intensify.

In order to experience a revival of the Bible in your personal life, it is important to take time each day to read, receive, and apply its truths to your life. James tells us that if we will continue in the perfect law of liberty — refusing to be forgetful hearers, but determined to be doers — we will be blessed in our ways. As you watch or listen to the programs in this series and work through this corresponding study guide, I trust you will search the Scriptures and allow the Holy Spirit to help you hear something new from God's Word that applies specifically to your life. I encourage you to be a doer of the Word He reveals to you. Whatever the cost, I assure you — it will be worth it.

> Thy words were found, and I did eat them;
> and thy word was unto me the joy and rejoicing of mine heart:
> for I am called by thy name, O Lord God of hosts.
> — Jeremiah 15:16

Your brother and friend in Jesus Christ,

Rick Renner

Unstoppable
Pressing Through Fear, Offense, and Negative Opinions To Fulfill God's Purpose

Copyright © 2022 by Denise Renner
1814 W. Tacoma St.
Broken Arrow, OK 74012

Published by Rick Renner Ministries
www.renner.org

ISBN 13: 978-1-6675-0260-1

eBook ISBN 13: 978-1-6675-0261-8

How To Use This Study Guide

This five-lesson study guide corresponds to *"Unstoppable" With Denise Renner* (**Renner TV**). Each lesson in this study guide covers a topic that is addressed during the program series, with questions and references supplied to draw you deeper into your own private study of the Scriptures on this subject.

To derive the most benefit from this study guide, consider the following:

First, watch or listen to the program prior to working through the corresponding lesson in this guide. (Programs can also be viewed at **renner.org** by clicking on the Media/Archives links or on our Renner Ministries YouTube channel.)

Second, take the time to look up the scriptures included in each lesson. Prayerfully consider their application to your own life.

Third, use a journal or notebook to make note of your answers to each lesson's Study Questions and Practical Application challenges.

Fourth, invest specific time in prayer and in the Word of God to consult with the Holy Spirit. Write down the scriptures or insights He reveals to you.

Finally, take action! Whatever the Lord tells you to do according to His Word, do it.

For added insights on this subject, it is recommended that you obtain Denise Renner's book *Unstoppable, Pressing Through Fear, Offense, and Negative Opinions To Fulfill God's Purpose.* You may also select from Rick and Denise's other available resources by placing your order at **renner.org** or by calling 1-800-742-5593.

TOPIC

Unstoppable to the End!

SCRIPTURES

Ephesians 4:16 *(KJV)* — From whom the whole body fitly joined together and compacted by that which every joint supplieth, according to the effectual working in the measure of every part, maketh increase of the body unto the edifying of itself in love.

Philemon 1:6 — That the sharing of your faith may become effective by the acknowledgment of every good thing which is in you in Christ Jesus.

SYNOPSIS

The five lessons in this study titled *Unstoppable* will focus on the following topics:

- **Unstoppable to the End!**
- **Unstoppable Against Offense**
- **Unstoppable Against the Negative Opinions of Others**
- **Unstoppable in the Face of Death**
- **Unstoppable Against All Odds**

The emphasis of this lesson:

You're a vital part in the Body of Christ and have a supply that others need and that no one else can give in quite the same way you can. God has designed and equipped you uniquely on purpose, because the people in your world need what He has placed in you. So don't get hung up on comparing yourself with others. Instead, embrace the way God has wired you and watch your one-of-a-kind supply touch the hearts and lives of others in amazing ways.

Today more than ever, we feel countless different pressures coming at us all the time, trying to stop us from running our race. These pressures can be anything from offense and the fear of man, to the power of other people's negative opinions, to a whole host of other obstacles. These types of roadblocks can stop you from running your God-given race, which is why it's so crucial to have an unstoppable attitude in Christ. When you do, you can press through fear, offense and negative opinions to fulfill the amazing purpose He has for you.

You Are Irreplaceably Needed in the Body of Christ

There is a calling that God has created especially, specifically, and intentionally for *you* to carry out. He placed that design and purpose inside you when you were in your mother's womb, even before you took your first breath. And every day since, the enemy has used different tools to try to stop you from fulfilling it.

One of the most common ways Satan does this is by trying to convince us of the lie that we're not valuable — but that couldn't be further from the truth! The Bible says in Ephesians 4:16 (*KJV*):

> **From whom the whole body fitly joined together and compacted by that which every joint supplieth, according to the effectual working in the measure of every part, maketh increase of the body unto the edifying of itself in love.**

How incredible is that? God says that every joint supplies something valuable and irreplaceable to the rest of the Body. Friend, you are a joint in the Body of Christ. Just to show you how important joints are, God created the human body with approximately 360 of them — our moving joints are what allow us to bend and walk and move freely.

When even one of your joints isn't working properly, life becomes much more difficult. You might need to take medications or have surgery to get that joint to do what it was designed to do, because each joint is vital to the health and growth of the rest of the body. In the same way, *you* are vitally important to the health and growth of the rest of the Body of Christ.

The Bible also says that you have a *supply* — a supply that is unlike anyone else's. God has called you to be *you*, not to compare yourself with or imitate anyone else. Whenever you compare yourself with somebody else, it's going to steal and diminish your own supply.

In the program, Denise shared how she experienced this firsthand because she used to do this with several people, even with her husband, Rick, who is an amazing Bible teacher. However, when she was habitually doing this, God began to show her that He didn't call her to teach or to be like Rick — He called Denise to be like *Denise*.

Likewise, God has not called you to be like somebody else — no matter how mature or "put together" or perfect that other person may seem — but to be *yourself*, the best version of *you* that you can be. When we make our goal to be like another person, we're diminishing and slowly shrinking the priceless gifts God has placed within us and the plan He has designed us to fulfill. When we compare ourselves to others, we can never ultimately measure up, because the standard we're using to gauge our success isn't the standard we were created to meet.

Don't Fall Into the Comparison Trap

Many years ago, when Rick and Denise were traveling full time in their teaching ministry in the United States, Denise was primarily concerned with preparing her music, taking care of their children, supporting her husband, and keeping the luggage intact, among other things. She was calmly focused on those tasks and the gifts God had placed within her... *until* she began comparing herself to someone else.

For example, whenever Rick and Denise would go to one particular church and she would observe the pastor's wife there, she would feel like a failure. This pastoring couple were really precious to them, but the wife appeared to be the epitome of a Proverbs 31 woman. This woman had a garden, made rugs, homeschooled her kids, and cooked and canned food frequently — it was like she had her domestic life totally together.

As a result, Denise felt as though she totally paled in this woman's shadow, and because Denise didn't do all the same things domestically, she *wasn't* a "Proverbs 31 woman." As Denise yielded to this nagging, tormenting feeling, it began to tear down her supply, her self-image, and her confidence — all because she had believed the lie from the enemy that she wasn't good enough.

One of Satan's biggest weapons against us as believers is the weapon of deception. If he can deceive you into believing that you don't have as much to give as somebody else, or that what you do have to give isn't important, then he can effectively deactivate the call and the power God has placed inside you. This is why it's so important to know and agree with the truth that God has spoken about you in His Word. You are a vital joint in the Body of Christ, you have an irreplaceable supply, and you've been created and equipped for a beautiful purpose (*see* Jeremiah 1:5).

The Power of Encouragement

Several years ago, Denise realized that she needed more confidence. She felt God's call and knew that she had gifts, but she also knew she needed to find a cheerleader. That person ended up being Terri Savelle Foy, and Terri and her ministry became Denise's daily dose of encouragement. Before long, Denise began to better recognize the ways God had gifted and called her, and she also began to see how agreeing with the enemy's bombarding thoughts of inadequacy had wrought so much "stoppable" power in her life.

Yet Denise knew that God's heart for all His children is for them to be truly UNstoppable.

One day as Terri was sharing her testimony, she said that for many years she hadn't used or stewarded her gifts or the knowledge God had put inside of her. One day she came to the realization, *I need to do something with what God has given me.* As Terri went on to pour her heart out, Denise wondered, *What if Terri had never recognized what was inside her? What if she never said, "I'm a joint. I'm valuable. I'm vital. I have a supply"?*

What if Terri had consequently never given out that supply to others? What if Denise had never gotten to hear her? Would others be watching Denise minister so boldly on television or be reading this lesson right now? Probably not.

This brings us to another question that is so important to think about: If you're not stepping out to be unstoppable in the giving of your supply, what's happening to the people in *your* life that aren't receiving what's in *you*? How might they be missing out on the precious gift that God wants to give through you?

Friend, it's so very important that we recognize the power of God in us, knowing that He didn't make a mistake in any part of the way He has wired us. When you were born again, He put His callings, His gifts, and

His Holy Spirit — the same power that raised Jesus from the dead (*see* Romans 8:11) — inside you. Our part is to recognize and agree with what God says about us, saying from our heart things like, "Yes, Lord. You said I'm vital — I believe I'm vital. You said I have a supply to give — I believe I have a supply to give. I may not know what it is yet, but I'm choosing to say yes to You and give whatever supply it is You've called me to give."

Say Yes to God

When you say *yes* to God, you open the door to the supply in you that somebody else desperately needs. The Bible says that as every part does its share — and that includes your share — it causes growth in the Body of Christ. And your part should not be compared to anyone else's. In fact, Second Corinthians 10:12 says that it's not wise to compare ourselves with others. When we do, it hinders us from giving what we have and robs someone else of the gift that we are meant to share with them.

By not giving what you have, someone else is doing without something that God wants to give them through you. You might think, *Well, I don't preach, I don't sing, I don't teach the Bible, I don't teach a Sunday School class…I don't do any of that stuff. What do I really have to offer?*

God has given each of us so many unique gifts, and each one is designed to meet a specific need in someone else's life. For instance, the gift of hospitality is a powerful one. Someone with this gift has the ability to invite you into his or her home, and the moment you walk in, you feel like burdens have been lifted off you. Guests can rest and be at peace because God has given that person the ability to create an environment where people can flourish.

What if you have the gift of giving? Who would be suffering if you didn't say yes to your gift of giving? What about the gift of mercy? Who would be going without if you didn't give from your heart the mercy that God gave you to share with others? No matter what your gift is, it is vitally important to say *yes* to God and to be obedient to share what He has placed inside you. Philemon 1:6 (*NKJV*) says that you need to acknowledge every good thing that's in you by Christ Jesus, so "that the sharing of your faith may become effective…."

God wants you to be aware of *every good thing* He has wired in you. When you're conscious of and sharing the supply He's placed inside of you, you're prepared to stand against the challenges and attacks of the enemy when they come. When others' negative opinions threaten your boldness, when fear of what others think wants to keep you from being authentic, and when offense attacks your heart, you can be prepared to fight back with the truth of God's Word.

Maybe you're thinking, *I've already been stopped. I've been stopped a long time because I've been so affected by what other people think.* Or maybe you're stuck in a loop, realizing, *I stopped a long time ago because I just can't get over what somebody did to me.* Well, there's good news for you! You have the Greater One living in you, and He's ready and willing to restore you, quicken you, and help you get your momentum back.

You have the resurrection power of Jesus inside you, and when you agree with who He says you are, you can fully be your unique self and bring the supply that only you were designed to give. When you lift your voice to the Lord, He recognizes *your* voice, because He has only given it to one person: *you.* Of the approximately seven billion people on the planet, no two of us have the same eyes, fingerprint, or voiceprint. Why? Because God wired us uniquely on purpose with a specific supply and a one-of-a-kind connection with Him.

You Are God's Stunningly Beautiful, Decorated Temple

Scripture says that "…we have this treasure in earthen vessels, that the excellency of the power may be of God, and not of us" (2 Corinthians 4:7 *KJV*). It says that we have a *treasure* inside of us.

Where the Renners live in Russia, there are so many amazing cathedrals decorated with gold and lapis and many other precious stones and mosaics that are truly magnificent. But as magnificent as they are, you are more decorated in your human spirit than those amazing cathedrals or even the most ornate building in the whole world.

God placed in you such amazing riches as a supply for you to give to others. Does the devil want to try to stop you? Yes, he does. He's intimidated by that treasure, that call, that supply on the inside of you, because he knows you are a threat to him and his plans. But because the Bible says that the One who lives inside you — Jesus — is greater than anything in this world, you can know you're equipped to conquer the enemy's attacks whenever they come (*see* 1 John 4:4).

It's time to be *unstoppable*! It's time to say *yes* to the Lord and *no* to the enemy's deception, others' negative opinions, the fear of man, and unforgiveness. All those have the power to stop us, but we have the power to override their influence.

So go forth and be unstoppable!

Denise's Prayer for You:

Lord Jesus, together we say "*YES*, I am going to push forward through whatever I need to, by Your grace and with Your strength. Thank You for giving me the grace to be unstoppable in fulfilling the calling You've given me, so that one day I can hear You say, 'Well done, My good and faithful servant.'"

Thank You for the power of the Holy Spirit inside my friend reading this prayer right now — that this person is agreeing with Your Word and opening the door for You to do great and mighty things in his or her life.

We worship and honor You as our God and the Lord of our lives. We give You all the praise for every good gift You've placed in us, and we trust You to show us how to share those gifts with others. In Jesus' name, amen.

STUDY QUESTIONS

Study to shew thyself approved unto God, a workman that needeth not to be ashamed, rightly dividing the word of truth.
— 2 Timothy 2:15

1. Who can you think of in Scripture that let comparison push him or her to make a terrible decision? How did it affect that person and God's plan for his or her life? Consider the example in First Samuel 8.
2. How does Scripture say we need to handle and use our God-given gifts? (*See* Matthew 5:14-16; Romans 12:6-8; 1 Peter 4:10,11.)

PRACTICAL APPLICATION

**But be ye doers of the word, and not hearers only,
deceiving your own selves.
— James 1:22**

1. Just like Denise found a cheerleader in Terri Savelle Foy, we each need to find a cheerleader to encourage us in our God-given supply, and we need to become a cheerleader to others. Who has God placed in your life as a cheerleader? Make it a goal to connect with them soon and enjoy the gift of their encouragement.

2. Who is one person you can reach out to and encourage this week? Ask God to show you how you can find and be a cheerleader in your everyday life.

3. Name at least one gift (talent or supply) that you know God has placed inside of you. Do you know of any others? How can you begin to share those gifts with the people around you?

TOPIC

Unstoppable Against Offense

SCRIPTURES

Matthew 18:21, 22 *(KJV)* — Then came Peter to him, and said, Lord, how oft shall my brother sin against me, and I forgive him? Till seven times? Jesus saith unto him, I say not unto thee, Until seven times: but, Until seventy times seven.

Matthew 18:28-30 — "But that servant went out and found one of his fellow servants who owed him a hundred denarii; and he laid hands on him and took him by the throat, saying, 'Pay me what you owe!' So his fellow servant fell down at his feet and begged him, saying, 'Have patience with me, and I will pay you all.' And he would not, but went and threw him into prison till he should pay the debt."

Matthew 18:34,35 — "And his master was angry, and delivered him to the torturers until he should pay all that was due to him. So My Heavenly

Father also will do to you if each of you, from his heart, does not forgive his brother his trespasses."

Ephesians 4:32 — And be kind to one another, tenderhearted, forgiving one another, even as God in Christ forgave you.

SYNOPSIS

The emphasis of this lesson:

One of the ways Satan will try to stop us from giving our supply is by trapping us with offense. Unforgiveness can affect our lives in terrible ways, but when we forgive, we set ourselves free from its prison, and we can finally enjoy life again!

In our last lesson, we talked about recognizing the power of God in us, and the importance of acknowledging this truth about ourselves: that we are a joint in the Body of Christ, and we have a necessary supply. Your supply is uniquely designed and crafted for you to give out, and it's so *one-of-a-kind* that it cannot be compared to anyone else's.

Remember, it's vitally important that we fulfill God's purpose for our lives. We begin to do this as we learn to live with the mindset, "God, I'm here. I recognize I'm a joint, and I believe I have a supply to give to this lost world where there's so much darkness. I can't wait to see how You give through me to help people today!"

Friend, you have a light to shine. You are vital to God's plan, and you have an amazing supply of gifts, talents, and abilities to give that will help others heal and encounter the love of Christ in the ways they need Him most.

But at the same time, you have an enemy who does NOT want you to discover, much less activate, the supply you've been given. He uses several different tools that can become powerful in stopping you — tools like offense, unforgiveness, bitterness, and resentment. In this lesson, we're going to focus on offense and why it's so crucial that we learn to forgive genuinely and to refuse to let grudges fester in our hearts.

The Damage Unforgiveness Can Do to Our Supply

Denise is so passionate about avoiding the trap of offense, because many years ago she had a terrible experience that led to unforgiveness, bitterness, and resentment. Whenever she tells the story, many people think, *How could that happen to Denise? She's married to a great minister, in ministry and called by God — this kind of stuff doesn't happen to people like that.* The truth is, it *does* happen to even those who walk with God and are powerfully involved in ministry, so it's incredibly important for all of us to be aware and prepared to deal with offenses when they come (*see* Luke 17:1).

Denise first began to realize something was wrong when she had painfully cold hands and feet all the time. Not only was she dealing with physical pain, but she was also facing mental torment, living in constant anxiety and even experiencing panic attacks. Denise felt completely trapped, because she would wake up with fearful thoughts and go to sleep with fearful thoughts. It seemed like there was no end to the fear. The only thing that would help her think clearly was going into a room by herself, turning on worship music and singing to God.

The situation became so intense that Denise's supply was stopped. This went on for a long time, and it was like being in a prison. She faced challenges with ministering to others and had almost no peace. She was still seeking Jesus, praying and reading the Word, but she had no practical answers or steps to take to get out of the trap she was in.

What Denise didn't know until later was that unforgiveness was ultimately causing these terrible symptoms. She simply didn't know that unforgiveness opens the door to the enemy to begin to work his strategies to steal, kill, and destroy in our lives. Denise truly didn't even realize that she had allowed unforgiveness into her life — she simply thought (as many of us do) that her problem was the person she was upset with, and that if that person would just change, everything would be okay.

However, you've probably lived enough life to know that ultimately we can't change other people. So when Denise couldn't change this other person, she wondered, *What am I supposed to do?*

One day after she and Rick had ministered in a large church and she had sung, someone came up to her and thanked her for singing. This individual also gave her the following prophetic word: "You're a very sensitive person; you've got a lot of broken places in your heart. But in twenty-four hours, you're going to wake up in a different world."

Thankfully, this person was right! Within 24 hours, God revealed to her that she had been holding on to unforgiveness and that she was bitter and resentful. Isn't it interesting that the Holy Spirit didn't show her anything about the other person, but instead showed her where *she* needed His grace to begin to function again, healed and whole, as the person He intended.

After Denise came to this realization and verbalized her forgiveness to the other person, she went soundly to sleep that night. When she woke up the next morning, she *was* in a different world! Her hands and feet were normal again, and her mind was finally clear. It was like Jesus had removed all the bitterness, resentment, and confusion from her heart and brought her back to a place of total peace and freedom.

There are so many people who are in the same situation that Denise used to be in — maybe you're finding yourself there right now. You know you've got gifts and callings inside you, but at some point, you were mistreated, hurt, and disappointed. This offense has caused you so much stress that you're dealing with symptoms in your own body and soul, and you're no longer effective in giving out the supply you were created to give.

We're Called To Forgive Generously

Jesus knew that unforgiveness and bitterness is "stoppable" material — it can stop us in our tracks from fulfilling the will of God — which is why He took it so seriously. He gave us the sobering statement in Matthew 6:14 and 15 that if we don't forgive, it shuts the door to our being able to receive His forgiveness.

Why would Jesus say that? Because He paid the ultimate price for our forgiveness. We're going to Heaven because of His forgiveness of our completely unpayable debt, and it's our job to pass on that forgiveness to others. When we do, we open the door to freedom for them, and we set ourselves free from the bondage of bitterness and resentment.

Let's look at Matthew 18:21 and 22 (*KJV*), another passage where Jesus is teaching about unforgiveness:

Then came Peter to him, and said, Lord, how oft shall my brother sin against me, and I forgive him? Till seven times? Jesus saith unto him, I say not unto thee, Until seven times: but, Until seventy times seven.

Peter initially says "seven times" because back in that day, Hebrews believed that if you managed to forgive someone three times in a day, that's really good. So Peter just added a few more to what he thought was already generous, thinking that would be perfect.

But Jesus upped the stakes by a long shot. He came back asking Peter — and us — to forgive "seventy times seven," or *490 times in a single day* if it's needed! Why would Jesus want us to forgive that many times every day? So we can live totally free of the prison of unforgiveness.

Jesus goes on to share a story that shows us the damage unforgiveness can do — not only does it put us in a mental/emotional prison, but it also causes us to put others in a kind of prison too. He illustrates this truth in one of His most impactful parables — the parable of the unforgiving servant (*see* Matthew 18:23-35). In it, Jesus tells us about a master and his servant who owed him a huge debt — the modern-day equivalent of about 269 million dollars. It was an utterly unpayable debt.

When this servant went to the master and begged him, saying, "Please don't put me and my family in prison! Just give me time, and I'll pay you everything," his master had compassion on him and forgave the debt. Not long after receiving this massive amount of mercy, this forgiven servant then went out and found a fellow servant who owed him the equivalent of just 20 dollars, demanding that he pay him back.

"But that servant went out and found one of his fellow servants who owed him a hundred denarii [or twenty dollars]; and he laid hands on him and took him by the throat, saying, 'Pay me what you owe [me]!'"
— Matthew 18:28

This forgiven servant had his hands around this other servant's neck, threatening him with prison if he didn't pay him back!

"So his fellow servant fell down at his feet and begged him, saying, 'Have patience with me, and I will pay you all [everything].' And he would not...."

— Matthew 18:29,30

The servant who had been forgiven a crippling, unpayable debt refused to forgive someone who owed him a trifle by comparison. As you read the rest of the passage, you'll discover he had been forgiven by the master of *so* much, but he refused to forgive a fellow servant of a very small, *miniscule* debt in comparison.

Verses 34 and 35 go on to tell the end of the story:

"And his master was angry, and delivered him to the torturers until he should pay all that was due to him. So My heavenly Father also will do to you if each of you, from his heart, does not forgive his brother his trespasses."

This parable is one of the hardest to swallow, but one of the most necessary to put into practice. It's easy to think, *But you don't know what they did to me. I've never been able to forgive — how can Jesus ask me to forgive someone who's hurt me so deeply?*

Well, one reason He can ask you to forgive is, when you were born again, He put the love of God — the ability to forgive — in your heart. You have the equipment from Him to set that person free of whatever he or she did to you.

Because you have God's love and grace, forgiveness is possible. It may be hard, it may take a long time — but with His help, you can forgive. Do others who hurt you owe you a debt? Yes, they do. Are they able to pay the debt? No. Were you able to pay the debt that you owed God? Again, no. But what did He do about it? He chose to forgive your debt.

Like the first servant in the story, we were completely unable to pay the debt that we owed God, but He chose to forgive us, anyway, and He calls us to do the same. Jesus doesn't ask us to deny the fact that others owe us a debt, but He wants us to release them from their debt. He wants to help us follow His example and extend that same forgiveness that He gave us. When we do, we experience life the way Jesus intended for us to live it — free, whole, and full of His grace for ourselves and others.

How Choosing To Forgive Sets You Free

Many years ago, when Denise was in a church in another country, she met a worship leader with a powerful story about the freedom that forgiveness can bring in our lives. This worship leader shared with Denise that she was married to her second husband. When Denise asked her what happened with her first husband, she shared her story.

This woman wasn't saved when she married her first husband, who eventually became an alcoholic. He abused her and their son so much that the son ended up having mental problems, so she divorced her husband.

After the divorce, the woman became saved and filled with the Holy Spirit, and ended up marrying her second husband, who was a believer. At that point, her life was very blessed, but the one circumstance that was still difficult was her son's continued battle with mental problems. She knew in her heart that she needed to forgive her ex-husband because Jesus forgave her, but seeing her son continue to live with those consequences every day made it incredibly hard. So she began to pray about it and seek the Lord for help.

One day she was cleaning out her apartment and had gathered a lot of trash in a huge pile. She was so excited because she felt like she was finally done, but then she looked over to another side of her apartment to see a little tiny piece of paper left. She was getting ready to discard it when the Holy Spirit started talking to her.

"You see this big pile of trash that you're so proud of?" He asked her. "Yes," she answered. He replied, "That's like the debt you owed Me. And that tiny little piece of paper? That's like the debt that your ex-husband owes you."

She said, "Oh Lord, I'm so sorry. I choose to forgive him; I release him for what he did." And that was the beginning of her process to forgive him. It wasn't easy, especially with watching her son's challenges, but she kept going and letting the Holy Spirit heal her heart and help her forgive. And in that process, something beautiful happened: God healed her son! She was also able to quit suspecting and accusing her second husband of the things that her ex had done (her new husband was a good man), so there was a lot more joy in their marriage.

Forgiveness Is Hard on the Flesh, But This Is What Jesus Asks Us To Do

When we don't forgive, it's like there's an invisible string connecting us to that other person. That person can be on the other side of the world, not even aware of how he or she hurt us, but if we hold on to the offense, no matter how long it has been, it's as if the wound happened "the day before"! We're still connected to it in our hearts by that invisible string of unforgiveness.

But when we choose to forgive, we cut that string and free ourselves from the connection to the offense. Jesus set us free and forgave our debt, the "millions of dollars" of debt that we could never pay. And those who owe us a debt they can't pay? We can free them of their debt, too, because we've been set free through His forgiveness. Ephesians 4:32 says:

> **And be kind to one another, tenderhearted, forgiving one another, even as God in Christ forgave you.**

You can free the people who've offended you by extending that same forgiveness you've received from God. What will happen when you free another person? You'll open the door of Heaven to your home, your relationships, etc. Jesus paid such a high price for you to have freedom and to be whole — please don't let unforgiveness rob you of that abundant life (*see* Isaiah 53:5; John 10:10). When you choose to walk out that forgiveness process with His help, you'll get to see how He blesses your life in new, beautiful ways.

Who in your life are you offended with? Do you feel stuck, like there's an invisible, unknown ceiling over your life that you haven't been able to identify? Ask the Holy Spirit to show you if perhaps it's an unresolved offense or unforgiveness. If it is, invite Him to help you begin the journey to forgive each person who has hurt you. Today is the day for you to get free from resentment and become the unstoppable person God created you to be.

Denise's Prayer for You:

Father, thank You for the wonderful presence of Your Spirit that's touching my friend right now. Please reveal any offenses we need to let go of and help us to release any offense, bitterness, or resentment that's been poisoning our lives. Thank You for searching and healing our hearts and giving us the grace to forgive a little more every day. We say *YES to You, Lord.*

Now say this out loud and let your heart agree:

I let go of offense and release _____ right now in Your name, Lord, and I ask You to help me continue to forgive until the process is complete. Thank You for forgiving me and for empowering me to forgive others so I can STAY free. In Jesus' name, amen.

STUDY QUESTIONS

Study to shew thyself approved unto God, a workman that needeth not to be ashamed, rightly dividing the word of truth.
— 2 Timothy 2:15

1. God's forgiveness is such a precious gift to us, but did you know He takes it even further? What does He do after He forgives us? (*See* Isaiah 43:25; Psalm 103:12; 1 John 1:9.)

2. What does Scripture say God does when we sincerely repent, whether to receive salvation or forgiveness after we've been saved? What attitude does He take toward us? (*See* Isaiah 55:7; Micah 7:18,19; Hebrews 4:15,16.)

3. It can be incredibly easy to have an unhealthy, critical attitude towards others, but why is it so important to avoid this bad habit? What do we need to remember about ourselves to have a more humble attitude? (*See* Luke 6:37; Matthew 5:7; 7:1-5; Ephesians 2:4,5; 4:32.)

PRACTICAL APPLICATION

But be ye doers of the word, and not hearers only, deceiving your own selves.
—James 1:22

1. Have you ever had challenges with forgiving someone? Who was, or is, it?

2. In light of this lesson, how do you want to handle the everyday opportunities that come up in life to be offended? Ask the Holy Spirit to help you grow in this area, to forgive small offenses as quickly as

possible, to help you work through forgiving those deeper hurts and to heal your heart from those wounds so you can be truly free from the prison of unforgiveness.

3. How might your life look different if you were able to live this out? Who/what would no longer have the power to trigger your emotions? In what situations would you be more peaceful than you've ever been? Where could you go that you haven't been able to go before in your walk with the Lord?

TOPIC

Unstoppable Against the Negative Opinions of Others

SCRIPTURES

1 Samuel 17:28-30 — "Why did you come down here? And with whom have you left those few sheep in the wilderness? I know your pride and the insolence of your heart, for you have come down to see the battle." And David said, "What have I done now?" Is there not a cause?" Then he turned...

1 Samuel 17:33-36 — "You are not able to go against this Philistine to fight with him; for you are a youth, and he a man of war from his youth." But David said to Saul, "Your servant used to keep his father's sheep, and when a lion or a bear came and took a lamb out of the flock, I went out after it and struck it, and delivered the lamb from its mouth; and when it arose against me, I caught it by its beard, and struck and killed it. Your servant has killed both lion and bear; and this uncircumcised Philistine will be like one of them, seeing he has defied the armies of the living God."

1 Samuel 17:43-46 — So the Philistine said to David, "Am I a dog that you come to me with sticks?" And the Philistine cursed David by his gods. And the Philistine said to David, "Come to me, and I will give your flesh to the birds of the air and the beasts of the field!" Then David said to the Philistine, "You come to me with a sword, with a spear, and with a javelin. But I come to you in the name of the Lord of hosts, the God of the armies of Israel, whom you have defied. This day the Lord will deliver you into my hand, and I will strike you and take your head from you. And this day I will give the carcasses of the camp of the Philistines to the birds of the air and the wild beasts of the earth, that all the earth may know that there is a God in Israel.

SYNOPSIS

The emphasis of this lesson:

Another tool the enemy uses to try and stop us is others' negative opinions. David had a sea of negative opinions thrown at him, but because he knew how to turn from them and not let criticism define him, he was courageous. He defeated Goliath and went on to ultimately fulfill his destiny — and *you* can fulfill your divine destiny too!

In the first lesson, we talked through the importance of recognizing that each of us is a vitally important joint in the Body of Christ, and we have a unique supply that no one else can bring to the table. When we remind ourselves over and over of this truth, we foil the enemy's plans to stop us, and we're able to keep giving our supply to those who need it.

Then in our second lesson, we learned how to recognize another thing that would try to stop us: the cycle of unforgiveness, bitterness, and resentment. As you learned from Denise's story, this cycle has the power to stop us right in the middle of our race, rob us of our momentum, and even cause negative mental, emotional, and physical symptoms. However, when we cooperate with Jesus and allow Him to help us forgive, we free ourselves from the prison of unforgiveness.

Today's lesson will help you overcome yet another obstacle that can stop you in your race: *others' negative opinions.*

Overcoming Others' Negative Opinions

How many times a day can we flash back to a moment when someone's hurtful words crushed us? How often do those memories turn into thoughts that make us doubt our character or our capability to do what we need to do? Many of us have thoughts like these frequently, and they usually sound something like:

- *Maybe I'm not good enough.*
- *I shouldn't have done/said that — what was I thinking?!!*
- *There's no way I can do this well.*
- *Am I even a good person? Or am I just pretending?*

It's incredibly easy to get stopped by thoughts of doubt from the world or the enemy that just keeps pressing on us, convincing us that we're not performing as we should.

The common denominator in all these thoughts is that they push us to adopt someone else's negative opinion of us, which usually has to do with our lacking something or being unable to do or give what's necessary in a situation. These faultfinding opinions come to all of us at some point — they even came to Jesus, who lived a perfect, sinless life!

In John chapter 7, we find a classic example of the massively different opinions people had about Jesus. One person says He was a devil, while another says He was good. Someone else claimed He was deceiving the people, and another said, "He's good; I believe in Him."

Yet another exclaimed, "How can He be so smart? I didn't know He studied!" while another critic asked, "Why hasn't He already been arrested?"

If you keep reading, the chatter goes on and on, opinions stacked on opinions, just like they do in our own lives. But that's all they are: *opinions.* Just because someone has an opinion doesn't make it truth — it simply makes it his opinion. Someone may even have a loud, strong opinion about us, but we don't have to accept it as a definition of who we are. We each have a race to finish, and holding on to others' criticism will only slow us down. But letting go of their words leaves us frees to run our race well.

Let Go of Criticism and Slay Your Giants!

Not only did Jesus understand this, but so did another amazing person in Scripture who had some negative opinions to overcome — and that person was David. He was surrounded by people telling him he was too small and just not good enough to fight Goliath (much less defeat him), but, thankfully, he threw their opinions aside and trusted God.

The story starts in First Samuel 17:28, where David's father Jesse asked him to leave their family's sheep with someone else and bring bread and other provisions of food to his brothers, who were with the rest of Israel's army.

As David arrived at the battlefield, he saw that the entire Israelite army was terrified of this one giant — Goliath, a champion on the Philistines' side who'd been defying and ridiculing God and His people for 40 days. Every morning, Goliath would demand that they send out a warrior from Israel to fight him man-to-man, but they were crippled with fear, so the war was at a stalemate. After taking stock of what was going on, David gave the provisions to his brothers and began asking questions.

"What will happen for the person who takes that giant down?" David asked. The soldiers around him then started to tell him about how King Saul had promised three things to whomever defeated Goliath: his daughter's hand in marriage, a huge fortune, and tax exemption for his whole family.

As David was asking his questions, his oldest brother Eliab saw him, became furious, and started accusing him, saying:

> **"Why did you come down here? And with whom have you left those few sheep in the wilderness? I know your pride and the insolence of your heart, for you have come down to see the battle."**
>
> **—1 Samuel 17:28**

Can you say Eliab was opinionated and critical! In their culture and time, Eliab, as the oldest son, had great authority over his little brother, yet it was David, the "runt of the litter," whom God had chosen to be the next king of Israel (*see* 1 Samuel 16). Eliab was most certainly jealous as he came in with his insulting, belittling, berating opinion of David.

But what did David do? More importantly, what did he choose *not* to do? David didn't engage in an argument or desperately try to defend himself. Instead, he gave a short response in verse 29:

> **And David said, "What have I done now? Is there not a cause?"**

Then in verse 30, we read that David chose to shift his focus.

Then he *turned*…

How many of us would have said something like, "Oh, my bad. I shouldn't have come out here! Probably should have stayed with the sheep…why did I open my mouth? Nobody wants me here anyway — even my own brother is trying to trash my reputation. What am I thinking? Forget the giant; I'm going home. It's not worth putting up with Eliab's nonsense."

Thank God that David didn't say that! He could have responded in so many ways to his brother's attacking words. He could have buckled out of fear that Eliab would keep trying to humiliate him. He could have turned the tables and started returning his accusations. He could have tried to defend himself or convince Eliab and everyone listening that his brother was wrong. But he chose the harder, better thing: He turned away from his brother's angry opinion and just kept going.

Then he had another negative opinion to deal with from an even higher authority: King Saul. In verse 33, he told David:

> **"You are not able to go against this Philistine to fight with him; for you are a youth, and he a man of war from his youth."**

David had already resisted and turned from his oldest brother's accusing opinion of him, but then King Saul definitively told him to his face, "You can't do this." Yet again, David had an opportunity to let someone else's opinion stop him from carrying out God's purpose. His response to Saul?

> **But David said to Saul, "Your servant used to keep his father's sheep, and when a lion or a bear came and took a lamb out of the flock, I went out after it and struck it, and delivered the lamb from its mouth; and when it arose against me, I caught it by its beard, and struck and killed it. Your servant has killed both lion and bear; and this uncircumcised Philistine will be like one of them, seeing he has defied the armies of the living God."**
>
> **— 1 Samuel 17:34-36**

What a faith-filled response! He remembered and shared how God had protected him in the past, essentially saying, "I respect you, but I have experience. I've already conquered a lion and a bear with God's help, and because I've been through both of those situations, I'm prepared to go and defeat Goliath."

David spoke with such authority and confidence that Saul tried to put his own armor on him and send him out to meet the giant! When the king's armor just wouldn't fit, David then had the courage to say, "No, I don't need your armor. God has equipped me with the supply I need. I'm going to be true to how He has created me and use the tools I'm familiar with." (*See* 1 Samuel 17:38-40.) And David stepped onto the battlefield, where yet *another* negative opinion was waiting for him: *Goliath's.*

> **So the Philistine said to David, "Am I a dog that you come to me with sticks?" And the Philistine cursed David by his gods. And the Philistine said to David, "Come to me, and I will give your flesh to the birds of the air and the beasts of the field!"**
> **—1 Samuel 17:43,44**

This was the giant's opinion. He was convinced David was nothing more than a bug to be squashed or a tally to add to his body count. But look at how David replied!

> **Then David said to the Philistine, "You come to me with a sword, with a spear, and with a javelin. But I come to you in the name of the Lord of hosts, the God of the armies of Israel, whom you have defied. This day the Lord will deliver you into my hand, and I will strike you and take your head from you. And this day I will give the carcasses of the camp of the Philistines to the birds of the air and the wild beasts of the earth, that all the earth may know that there is a God in Israel.**
> **—1 Samuel 17:45,46**

David reminded everyone that he had something behind him so much more powerful than all the negative opinions others had been throwing at him: He had the backing of the Lord of Hosts Himself! It was His opinion and His power that David recognized in that defining moment, and he went on to win the defining victory of his life.

What About You?

Have you been affected by other people's negative opinions of you? Did you ever stop doing what you were doing because someone like Eliab criticized your motives or your ability? Maybe they said things like, "You're not equipped for that. Remember how you tried last time and failed? You'll probably fail this time too, so why put out the effort?" Or maybe you heard opinions like, "Oh, you tried to get free of that addiction before, but you just got sucked back in — don't waste your energy on trying again."

No matter what others have said about you, you don't need to defend yourself or try to prove them wrong. Like David, you can simply turn and keep going on the path God has for you. That's the most powerful response to criticism there is — to successfully fulfill the plans and purposes of God for your life.

Whose opinion do you need to turn from? Maybe for you, it's not another person in your life telling you that you're going to fail, but the enemy or your own reasoning is telling you that you don't have what it takes. If you have your own negative opinion of yourself to overcome, today is the day to invite God to transform your thinking so you can see yourself the way He does and know His will for your life (*see* Romans 12:2). Once you do, you can turn from the voice of that inner critic and wholeheartedly pursue the destiny He has for you.

Let's review for a minute. When negative opinions came against Jesus, what did Jesus do? He **ignored** them and kept moving forward in ministry. What did David do? The Bible says David **turned away** from them and **remembered** how God had been faithful in the past.

In the same way, it's so important for us to remember what God has done in the past and how He has been faithful to equip us and bring us through hard situations.

This idea of remembering the struggles God has brought us through is confirmed in Romans 5:3 and 4, which says that the challenges we face ultimately produce *character* in us, and that character produces *hope*, or a confident expectation of what God will do again and again in your life as you look to Him and trust Him.

If you've had an experience with God in which He intervened in your life, take time to remember it. Walk through how you felt before and after He made a way for you. Think about how He healed your body, connected you with the right person or resource, or provided finances when you were in a desperate situation. Maybe He calmed your mind when you were dealing with anxiety, or delivered a loved one from an addiction that you thought he would never escape.

Even if only one small act of kindness from a stranger comes to mind, focus on that for a moment. Whatever God has done in your life, remembering it can reinforce your faith like nothing else. For David, as he was preparing to face Goliath, remembering how the Lord had empowered him to rescue his lambs from a lion and a bear was like fuel on the fire of his boldness. And the same God who strengthened him then is the same God who will strengthen you now — He's the same yesterday, today, and forever (*see* Hebrews 13:8). Let His faithfulness give you courage!

Like Jesus and like David, let us turn from the negative opinions of others and say yes to God, because He is the best Partner you'll ever have against the challenges of life. And when we say yes to Him, His resurrection power in us makes the impossible possible, and the stoppable unstoppable! When we yield to His Spirit and receive His grace, we can function as the joint we are in the Body of Christ, and we'll have the power to give out that vitally important, one-of-a-kind, giant-defeating supply.

If there was ever a time for us to be committed to keeping our focus on Jesus and not being distracted by the world's criticism, it is *right now*. It's time for us to be unstoppable in fulfilling the purpose God has for our lives.

Denise's Prayer for You:

Father, I thank You for my amazing friend who's going through this study right now, and for what You're doing inside of this person's heart. May we become more and more committed to what it is You've called us to do. Give us the ability to ignore, turn away from, and override the criticism of other people so that we can remain unstoppable. With Your help, we can refuse to let offense, unforgiveness, or even others' negative opinions stop us from running our race effectively. Thank You for giving us Your Spirit to remind us of truth, to see ourselves the way You see us, and to help us continue on the path You have for us, even when it's hard. In Jesus' name, amen.

STUDY QUESTIONS

Study to shew thyself approved unto God, a workman that
needeth not to be ashamed, rightly dividing the word of truth.
— 2 Timothy 2:15

1. Take a look at First Samuel 16:1-13, taking note of the process Samuel went through as he was looking for the next person to anoint as king of Israel. What did God say about Eliab and the rest of David's brothers? What can we learn from this about what God prioritizes when He's looking for someone to anoint for a task?

2. Now read the rest of First Samuel 16. What was the context of how David was originally introduced to Saul? How do you think this influenced Saul's opinion of David's capability?

PRACTICAL APPLICATION

But be ye doers of the word, and not hearers only,
deceiving your own selves.
— James 1:22

1. Have you ever had an Eliab in your life? Maybe it was literally an older sibling or a jealous coworker, classmate, or someone who served on the same ministry team as you. What did that person say about you that you still remember to this day? Ask God to help you forgive him or her and release that negative opinion of you so you can turn away from it and discover the truth about what He has called and equipped you to do.

2. Now for the harder question: Have you ever *been* an Eliab in someone else's life? What do you wish you had that he or she seemed to have? This can be a hard possibility to think about, but it's so important. The enemy would love for you to waste your energy on jealousy and lashing out at others, but God wants so much more for you. Think about what it is you're likely to envy in others, and bring the hurt that's associated with it to Jesus. He wants to heal your heart from disappointment and give you the grace to cheer others on as you're waiting for Him to fulfill the desires of your own heart.

TOPIC

Unstoppable in the Face of Death

SCRIPTURES

2 Kings 4:25-32 — And so she departed, and went to the man of God at Mount Carmel. So it was, when the man of God saw her afar off, that he said to his servant Gehazi, "Look, the Shunammite woman! Please run now to meet her, and say to her, 'Is it well with you? Is it well with your husband? Is it well with the child?'" And she answered, "It is well." Now when she came to the man of God at the hill, she caught him by the feet, but Gehazi came near to push her away. But the man of God said, "Let her alone; for her soul is in deep distress, and the Lord has hidden it from me, and has not told me." So she said, "Did I ask a son of my lord? Did I not say, 'Do not deceive me'?" Then he said to Gehazi, "Get yourself ready, and take my staff in your hand, and be on your way. If you meet anyone, do not greet him; and if anyone greets you, do not answer him; but lay my staff on the face of the child." And the mother of the child said, "As the Lord lives, and as your soul lives, I will not leave you." So he arose and followed her. Now Gehazi went on ahead of them, and laid the staff on the face of the child; but there was neither voice nor hearing. Therefore he went back to meet him, and told him, saying, "The child has not awakened." When Elisha came into the house, there was the child, lying dead on his bed.

2 Kings 4:34-37 — And he went up and lay on the child, and put his mouth on his mouth, his eyes on his eyes and his hands on his hands; and he stretched himself out on the child, and the flesh of the child became warm. He returned and walked back and forth in the house, and again went up and stretched himself out on him; then the child sneezed seven times, and the child opened his eyes. And he called Gehazi and said, "Call this Shunammite woman." So he called her. And when she came in to him, he said, "Pick up your son." So she went in, fell at his feet, and bowed to the ground; then she picked up her son and went out.

Romans 8:11 — But if the Spirit of Him who raised Jesus from the dead dwells in you, He who raised Christ from the dead will also give life to your mortal bodies through His Spirit who dwells in you.

SYNOPSIS

The emphasis of this lesson:

In the story of Elisha and the Shunammite woman, we learn how our determination to pursue the presence of Jesus can help us experience breakthrough. You have the resurrection power of God inside of you, and He wants to bring your dead dreams back to life.

Throughout the last three lessons, we've discovered how important it is for us to remember our value in the Body of Christ and refuse to let unforgiveness, insecurity, or the negative opinions of others stop us from running our race well. God has a purpose, a call, and a plan for each of our lives — and for us to fulfill that plan, we need to have an unstoppable attitude to overcome the roadblocks that the enemy tries to place in our path.

For this lesson, we're going to focus on one of the most incredible, faith-filled women in Scripture who had an unstoppable attitude: the Shunammite woman in 2 Kings 4.

A Dream Given

Her story begins with the Old Testament prophet Elisha, who would come to her city every so often, and whenever he did, she would go out of her way to welcome and care for this man of God. Because the Holy Spirit wasn't given to indwell every person yet, the only presence of God that humans could experience was when they came close to a prophet or mighty man of God, such as a priest or king. This woman was so hungry for God's presence that she was willing to do whatever it took to be close to Elisha.

Knowing that, this Shunammite and her husband decided to start preparing meals for Elisha whenever he passed through their area. Not long after that, she said to her husband, "Let's build a room so that when Elisha comes this way, we can invite him to come stay with us."

Soon they built a room for Elisha, who was so touched by her generosity that he and his servant Gehazi asked her, "You've been so kind to us — what can we do for you? Can we put in a good word for you with the king or the commander of the army?" She replied with a simple, "No, thank you," explaining that she had a home among her own people and had no such need.

Gehazi then said to Elisha, "You know, her husband is old and they don't have any children." Elisha then asked him to call the Shunammite woman back in and he told her, "This time next year, you will be holding a son in your arms." At first, she didn't dare get her hopes up that Elisha was right. She had been barren so many years that she surely thought it was impossible for her to have a child.

Yet that's exactly what happened! She had a miraculous pregnancy, a miraculous birth, and a son in her arms a year later. Can you imagine the joy this woman and her husband had about this little one, especially after so many years of childlessness? He must have been the light and pride and joy of his parents' lives, and very well loved and wanted.

A Dream Lost

The little boy grew, and one day as he was out working with the reapers and his father during a harvest, the little boy grabbed his head and cried out in great pain from an intense headache. His father asked one of their servants to take him home to his mother. The little boy was taken to the Shunammite woman and laid in her lap, and at noon, her son died tragically in her arms (*see* 2 Kings 4:18-20).

It was then that she made a powerful, unstoppable decision based solely on faith. She took her son up to Elisha's room, laid him on Elisha's bed and closed the door. She didn't tell anyone that her son had died, but instead told one of their servants to saddle a donkey for her to go see Elisha. She wasn't planning for a funeral — she was planning for a resurrection.

> **And so she departed, and went to the man of God at Mount Carmel. So it was, when the man of God saw her afar off, that he said to his servant Gehazi, "Look, the Shunammite woman! Please run now to meet her, and say to her, 'Is it well with you? Is it well with your husband? Is it well with the child?'" And she answered, "It is well."**
>
> **— 2 Kings 4:25, 26**

Can we just take a moment to appreciate her amazing response? This precious woman had just lost the dream most dear to her heart, yet she still said, "It is well with me." What kind of faith and determination did it take for her to answer that way?

> **Now when she came to the man of God at the hill, she caught him by the feet, but Gehazi came near to push her away. But the man of God said, "Let her alone; for her soul is in deep distress, and the Lord has hidden it from me, and has not told me." So she said, "Did I ask a son of my lord? Did I not say, 'Do not deceive me'?" Then he said to Gehazi, "Get yourself ready, and take my staff in your hand, and be on your way. If you meet anyone, do not greet him; and if anyone greets you, do not answer him; but lay my staff on the face of the child." And the mother of the child said, "As the Lord lives, and as your soul lives, I will not leave you." So he arose and followed her.**
> **— 2 Kings 4:27-30**

This woman was so determined, she refused to take a staff sent to her child as an answer, because it would be a lower-level version of what she was seeking: God's presence and power resting on Elisha. We see this in her words to Elisha as she fell at his feet and exclaimed, "As the Lord lives and as your soul lives, I will not leave you."

In the same way, we have to be relentless in our pursuit of Jesus' presence and power in our lives. There are many times in life when someone will offer you a lower-level answer with an appearance of help in it, but there won't be any genuine power or substance. Remember, you're seeking the bona fide resurrection power of God to manifest itself in your situation, not a cheap copy or imitation of the things of God.

The Shunammite wasn't going to settle for just a hint of God's presence and power — she was determined to have the real deal, and it's a good thing she was!

A Dream Restored

> **Now Gehazi went on ahead of them, and laid the staff on the face of the child; but there was neither voice nor hearing. Therefore he went back to meet him, and told him, saying, "The child has**

not awakened." When Elisha came into the house, there was the child, lying dead on his bed.

— 2 Kings 4:31,32

When you need a resurrection, you can't afford to be satisfied with the lower-level answer. If you're needing a miracle, whether it's in your marriage, your health, your finances, or anything else, you have to get to a place where you're believing, "God has answers for me, and I'm not letting go until I get those answers from Him — I'm not settling for a shadow of His presence." (*See* Hebrews 11:6.)

Denise also had to come to this point in her walk with God. Not long before she received the prophetic word from that worship leader in Russia that she would wake up in 24 hours in a new world, she made a similar determination. Waking up in the middle of the night, exhausted, full of anxiety, and in physical pain that had lasted for months, she prayed, "God, I am *going* to hear from You. I don't know what You're doing, I don't know what's going on, and I don't know why I'm going through this, *but I am not letting go of YOU*."

It was just a few weeks later that her answer came through that prophetic word. When she took action based on God's direction to forgive, she was set free from the terrible symptoms that had been robbing her of her ability to enjoy life and fulfill God's plan. Similarly, we need to have that "come-hell-or-high-water" commitment to seek God until we have an answer.

That was the attitude of this incredible Shunammite woman, which is why Elisha came to her home — because she was *persistent*.

> And he went up and lay on the child, and put his mouth on his mouth, his eyes on his eyes and his hands on his hands; and he stretched himself out on the child, and the flesh of the child became warm. He returned and walked back and forth in the house, and again went up and stretched himself out on him; then the child sneezed seven times, and the child opened his eyes. And he called Gehazi and said, "Call this Shunammite woman." So he called her. And when she came in to him, he

said, "Pick up your son." So she went in, fell at his feet, and
bowed to the ground; then she picked up her son and went out.
— 2 Kings 4:34-37

The last time this determined mother had held her son in her arms, he
was dead. Out of complete faith, she had put his lifeless body on Elisha's
bed, closed the door, and sought out a miracle. The next time she held
her son, he was alive and well again. That's the resurrection power of God —
the same power present through the Holy Spirit that lives in you and me
right now because we've been born again of that same Spirit.

What Do You Need To Have Resurrected?

Is there anything sweeter than deciding to be unstoppable? To push
through offense and forgive; to push through the fear of others'
disapproval and negative opinions; to take hold of God and refuse to
let go until you receive what you need. That's what happened for the
Shunammite woman — she refused to take no for an answer — and the
same thing can happen for you.

So, in a manner of speaking, what has "died" in your arms?

Maybe it was your marriage, maybe it was a dream for ministry or a
certain career path, maybe it was something that you believed God was
telling you to do, but things just fell apart and it seemed like all hope was
lost.

Whatever you've lost, you're still believing God can show up in your situation. If you weren't, you wouldn't be taking the time to study His Word
or go through this study. You're still believing and you're still pushing
through because you have the Holy Spirit and the resurrection power of
Jesus living inside you, and He has kept a seed of hope alive in your heart.
We can see this amazing truth echoed in Romans 8:11, which says:

> But if the Spirit of Him who raised Jesus from the dead dwells
> in you, He who raised Christ from the dead will also give life to
> your mortal bodies through His Spirit who dwells in you.

Together, let's begin to look at our situations with hope. When the
enemy tries to stop us in our tracks and says, *You're not going any further*,
let's choose to push back. Let's agree with what God says about us and
declare, "NO, I *will* go further. God didn't bring me this far to only come

this far. I refuse to be stopped. He provides me with everything I need, and by His grace I will push through until I see His resurrection power come into my situation!"

As we do this, we open the door for Him to show up and show off in our lives in the most incredible ways — so let's press on!

Denise's Prayer for You:

Father, thank You for Your presence inside each of us, including my friend reading this right now. Together, we agree with You that Your Spirit and Your power live in us, so we *can* be unstoppable. We believe that with Your help, we're going to move forward through these difficult times and situations, and that You're with us to comfort and teach us every step of the way to the other side. We seek You as our source of answers and of life, because You alone can resurrect what has died in us. Father, we give You all the praise for Your faithfulness in loving and caring for us, and we thank You for Your mercies that are new every morning. In Jesus' name, amen.

STUDY QUESTIONS

Study to shew thyself approved unto God, a workman that
needeth not to be ashamed, rightly dividing the word of truth.
— 2 Timothy 2:15

1. Read Second Kings 4:8 and notice where Elisha *is* and where he *isn't*. Is he in Israel or outside Israel? How does knowing the Shunammite woman and her husband were actually foreigners living in another land impact your perception of the story?
2. When the Shunammite woman went to find Elisha, the Bible says he was at Mount Carmel. What other amazing event happened at Mount Carmel? (Hint: Read 1 Kings 18:16-45 to find out.)

PRACTICAL APPLICATION

But be ye doers of the word, and not hearers only,
deceiving your own selves.
—James 1:22

1. Like the Shunammite woman and her husband, we need to create space for and welcome God's presence in our lives through the way we live our lives. Lean in and ask the Holy Spirit, *What would make You feel more welcome in my life?* Take a moment to journal what He says, and ask Him to help you begin to take those steps today.

2. As we asked in this lesson, what has died in your arms? Which God-given dreams, relationships, or hopes feel buried and gone forever? What could your life look like if they were resurrected? Bring them to Jesus, asking Him to do what only He can do, and watch Him breathe fresh life into them and *you.*

3. Do you have the determination of the Shunammite woman? If so, your faith is amazingly strong!! If not, ask God to impart the determination and boldness you need to keep asking, seeking, and knocking until He intervenes (*see* Matthew 7:7,8).

LESSON 5

TOPIC

Unstoppable Against All Odds

SCRIPTURES

Romans 8:11 — But if the Spirit of Him who raised Jesus from the dead dwells in you, He who raised Christ from the dead will also give life to your mortal bodies through His Spirit who dwells in you.

Matthew 15:24 — …"I was not sent except to the lost sheep of the house of Israel."

Matthew 15:26-28 — But He answered and said, "It is not good to take the children's bread and throw it to the little dogs." And she said, "Yes, Lord, yet even the little dogs eat the crumbs which fall from their masters' table." Then Jesus answered and said to her, "O woman, great is your faith! Let it be to you as you desire." And her daughter was healed from that very hour.

Acts 1:8 — "But you shall receive power when the Holy Spirit has come upon you; and you shall be witnesses to Me in Jerusalem, and in all Judea and Samaria, and to the end of the earth."

SYNOPSIS

The emphasis of this lesson:

In the story of the Canaanite woman, we find out that some of life's biggest obstacles require endurance, perseverance, and incredibly humble faith to see God's intervention. Your persistence in prayer makes a massive difference, both in your life and in the lives of others.

Over the course of this series, we've begun to recognize and combat a few of the enemy's biggest tactics to stop us from running our race, especially offense and the fear of people and their negative opinions. All of these can have "stopping power" in our lives, but like we discovered in Lesson 4, we have something so much more formidable in us: the resurrection power of Jesus Christ, which we're promised in Romans 8:11.

> **But if the Spirit of Him who raised Jesus from the dead dwells in you, He who raised Christ from the dead will also give life to your mortal bodies through His Spirit who dwells in you.**

Think for a moment about just how amazing that power is. The same Spirit who raised Jesus from the dead lives in *you*. We all need this revelation to be real in our hearts — we need to be convinced that this unstoppable power not only exists, but that we have access to it through the mighty Holy Spirit.

When we are born again by the grace of God — not by our actions or good deeds — His Spirit and power come to live in us. After we're saved, even though we can't physically see His Spirit, we are blessed and can experience His saving power in our lives because we believe and persistently seek Him (*see* John 20:29; Luke 18:1-8; 2 Timothy 1:7; Ephesians 3:20).

The Faith of Another Desperate, Determined Mom

In this final lesson, we're going to talk about one more woman who was unstoppable in her faith. She kept pushing through years of obstacles, opportunities to be offended, and others' negative opinions until she had the breakthrough she needed from Jesus.

We find her story in Matthew 15, where we learn that like the woman from Shunem in Lesson 4, she was actually not from Israel either. She was from Canaan, which means that her ancestors had been enemies of God's people. The Canaanites were known for human sacrifices and worshipping idols, so by any Jewish person's standard, she came from a terrible background.

Yet in spite of others' negative opinions of her, she pushed through crowds of Jews and cried out to Jesus for help. Over and over, she shouted, "Have mercy on me, O Lord, Son of David! My daughter is severely demon-possessed." (*See* Matthew 15:22.)

What in the world would make this foreign woman so bold as to continually shout to get Jesus' attention? Two things: *belief* and *desperation*. She knew and believed that Jesus was her only answer, and she was desperate for her daughter to be set free from the demon that was running her life.

Let's think for a minute about what this precious girl and her mom were going through. We know when the Bible describes demon possessions, it often includes symptoms like foaming at the mouth, cutting oneself, being thrown into fire, or water and even living among tombs. Horrible things were happening to this little girl, and neither she nor her mother could do anything to stop it.

Can you imagine being in this woman's shoes? If your mom or dad, brother or sister, son or daughter, or someone else you love dearly was being tormented day and night by the enemy, wouldn't you cry out to Jesus for His mercy?

Oftentimes when we do find ourselves in a position like this, in which we're interceding for someone else, it can be really difficult to keep praying when the answer takes a long time to come. Yet that's what this Canaanite woman did.

She had a tremendous desire to see her daughter made well, and that desperate longing overrode her fear of what others would think. She knew who she was, who her ancestors were, and that Jewish people were likely to reject her, but she refused to let that stop her. She kept crying out so much that the disciples were asking Jesus to send her away.

But guess what? She was still totally unmoved. Then Jesus answered her cries with the following surprising response.

> ..."I was not sent except to the lost sheep of the house of Israel."
>
> —Matthew 15:24

What a potentially disheartening response! Yet, again, this woman kept pressing through the crowd, falling at Jesus' feet, and worshipping Him, saying, "Lord, help me." She refused to give up, so she kept pursuing Jesus, knowing He was her only answer.

God Honors Persistence

When we want and need something from God, how many of us really know and believe that He's our *only* answer? How often do we settle for a lower-level answer coming from another flawed human, or even our own reasoning, just because we didn't get a real answer from Him fast enough?

How different could our lives look if we would pursue and worship Jesus relentlessly, like this woman from Canaan? What kind of grace could we receive from Him if we would keep praying this simple, sincere, worshipful prayer, "Lord, help me"? Pursuing and honoring Jesus as our only answer allows us to exchange our worries and our challenges for His presence, even when some situations require greater perseverance from us.

That's exactly where this woman was — in a situation that called for great endurance. In the next few verses, we see just how persistent she was.

> But He answered and said, "It is not good to take the children's bread and throw it to the little dogs." And she said, "Yes, Lord, yet even the little dogs eat the crumbs which fall from their masters' table."
>
> —Matthew 15:26,27

This is the first time in Scripture where Jesus talks about bread as a symbol of healing, more specifically calling healing "the children's bread" and essentially calling this mother a "little dog." *OUCH!* But this amazingly tenacious woman knows that at the same table where the children eat their bread, the little dogs under the table watch for and catch the falling crumbs.

Even when Jesus said something that sounded a lot like an insult, she still responded with a humble faith that healing was available for her daughter, believing that even a metaphorical "crumb" was enough to set her completely free. This is the kind of unstoppable faith *we* want to develop!

Let's read this mother's response again.

> **And she said, "Yes, Lord, yet even the little dogs eat the crumbs which fall from their masters' table."**
> **—Matthew 15:27**

She was essentially saying, "Jesus, I know I'm not of the lost sheep of the house of Israel. I know I'm a Canaanite woman, but if healing is the bread on the table, and Your people are the children eating the bread, then I can be the puppy under the table that catches the crumbs. I know You're able to heal, and even a crumb of Your healing is exactly what my daughter needs."

Finally, breakthrough came!

> **Then Jesus answered and said to her, "O woman, great is your faith! Let it be to you as you desire." And her daughter was healed from that very hour.**
> **—Matthew 15:28**

This little girl never saw Jesus or heard His voice, but because of her mom's incredible, persistent faith, she was delivered from the enemy's oppression in her life. Isn't that powerful?

Your Unstoppable Faith Makes a Difference

Have you ever been moved or stopped by other people's opinions? There were *so many opinions* surrounding this Canaanite woman. First of all, Jesus ignored her. Second, she was crying out so much that even the disciples asked Jesus to tell her to leave! Third, she was in a crowd of Jews who most definitely thought she didn't deserve to be there at all.

Despite all these things, this woman got her miracle because she refused to give up. She saw that Jesus was her only answer, would not let go of her faith, and didn't take no for an answer. She didn't even get offended when Jesus appeared to initially say no — or when the disciples wanted to send her away. She knew that He was her only answer, and she didn't quit until she got what she came for. She was truly unstoppable.

Do you have that kind of determination to get what you need from Jesus? Are you set on pushing through all the obstacles the devil's been trying to put in your way? If not, Jesus wants to help you. He paid the highest price for us to overcome those obstacles, and He's prepared to lead and empower you every step of the way.

Here's another question to think about: When we worship Him, do we really give Him our doubts and pain and fear so we can grab hold of His presence and receive His peace? The attitude of our hearts needs to be, "Lord, You're My only answer, so I'm coming to You. I exchange my worry, I exchange my care, I exchange my doubt, I exchange my fear — all for You and Your presence. I receive You and look to and acknowledge You as my only answer. Lord, help me."

When we give Him this kind of sincere worship, it opens our heart to pray simply and with faith. Knowing that He hears us, we can cry out, "Lord, help me," and He will answer (*see* John 16:24; Hebrews 11:6; 1 John 5:14).

Who are you interceding for right now? Maybe you're like the Canaanite woman, crying out desperately for an answer for your son or daughter. Maybe a loved one has lost his or her job, or your coworker has just been diagnosed with a serious illness. Or maybe there's someone you care about who hasn't received Jesus yet, and that's weighing on your heart.

Whatever you're facing, Jesus promised that He has already conquered it, and since He's in you, you have what it takes to push through, to not quit, and to finish your race with joy (*see* Psalm 18:29; John 16:33; Hebrews 12:1,2; 1 John 4:4).

It's God's ultimate, perfect plan that we get to be part of, His calling that we're pursuing, and the race that He's marked out for us that we're running. He has promised to guide and strengthen us by His Spirit all the way to the end, so we don't have to worry about figuring out everything in this life on our own (*see* Isaiah 41:10; 58:11; Matthew 28:20; 2 Timothy 1:7). Thank God for His empowering grace!

He says in Acts 1:8:

> **"But you shall receive power when the Holy Spirit has come upon you; and you shall be witnesses to Me in Jerusalem, and in all Judea and Samaria, and to the end of the earth."**

He has given you this unstoppable power on the inside to enable you to come through every roadblock the enemy throws at you and to emerge victorious on the other side.

Friend, it is certainly *not* a mistake that you are living right now, at this moment in history (*see* Esther 4:14). God, in His infinite wisdom and strategy, chose you to live in the place, time, and circle of people that you interact with *on purpose*.

Before the foundation of the world, He decided when you would be born, and He has placed you here and now. Why? Because here and now is exactly when and where your unique supply is destined to make a difference. You are truly a world changer. Your voice, your supply, your gift, your ability, and your heart are so very needed right now. And God wants you to be unstoppable.

I encourage you to go forth and conquer all that He has created you to overcome!

Denise's Prayer for You:

Father, I thank You so much for Your power and Your Spirit in my friend, and that through You, this precious person has the power to push through every obstacle, difficulty, and terrible situation he or she is facing right now. Thank You for guiding, empowering, and comforting this person's heart, and for making my friend truly unstoppable. May this one that is so dear to Your heart know just how much You love him or her, and that Your power is greater than every pressure he or she will ever face in the world. Father, You are totally faithful, so we look to You as our only answer, believing and watching for the breakthrough we need. We look forward with joy to all the ways You will help us keep persevering. Thank You for Your powerful, life-giving, peace-producing presence in our lives, and that You've promised to stay with us through every step of our race. In Jesus' name, amen.

STUDY QUESTIONS

Study to shew thyself approved unto God, a workman that **needeth not to** be ashamed, rightly dividing the word of truth.
— 2 Timothy 2:15

1. The faith of the Canaanite woman in the story we read today is truly incredible, and without a doubt, challenges us to grow in our own faith like never before. Who else came to Jesus with mountain-moving faith? What similarities do you see in that story and the Canaanite woman's story? (*Hint*: read Matthew 8:5-13.)

2. Who is one other woman in the New Testament who came to Jesus with wildly persistent faith (*see* Mark 5:25-34)? What was her need? How did Jesus respond? What attitude did she, the Canaanite woman, and the Roman centurion all have in common?

PRACTICAL APPLICATION

But be ye doers of the word, and not hearers only, deceiving your own selves.
— James 1:22

1. Like the Canaanite woman, sometimes we have opportunities to be offended at God when He doesn't respond how or when we would have hoped. When that happens, it can be incredibly hard to keep believing that His love and compassion for us are really present. What is one thing you've asked God for that has been delayed? Take a minute to write it down. Invite the Holy Spirit to heal your heart from the wound of that disappointment. Ask Him to help you see the situation from His perspective and give you the grace you need to have tenacious faith again. Know that He will come through for you in the time and in the ways you need it most.

2. Are there others who have had tenacious faith praying for you? What breakthrough happened in your life as a result? Spend a few minutes thinking about the way God put you on their heart, led them to pray, gave them grace to keep praying, and how He intervened on your behalf. If you can, reach out and thank them for their persistence. Remind them of how they were such a part of your breakthrough. Even if you're not able to get in touch with them, take a moment to thank God for hearing their prayers.

3. Lastly, who is someone you love that needs to be fought for in prayer, like the Canaanite woman's daughter? What hard thing is that person facing right now? Make a game plan to begin to pray for that person consistently, maybe even set a timer on your phone to remind you. Then watch with eyes of faith for God to show up and show off in that person's life.

Notes

Notes

CLAIM YOUR FREE RESOURCE!

As a way of introducing you further to the teaching ministry of Rick Renner, we would like to send you free of charge his teaching CD, "How To Receive a Miraculous Touch From God."

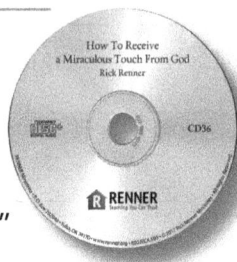

In His earthly ministry, Jesus commonly healed *all* who were sick of *all* their diseases. In this profound message, learn about the manifold dimensions of Christ's wisdom, goodness, power, and love toward all humanity who came to Him in faith with their needs.

☑ **YES, I want to receive Rick Renner's monthly teaching letter!**

Simply scan the QR code to claim this resource or go to:
renner.org/claim-your-free-offer

Connect

WITH US!

R renner.org   f facebook.com/rickrenner

▶ youtube.com/rennerministries   instagram.com/rickrrenner

www.ingramcontent.com/pod-product-compliance
Lightning Source LLC
Chambersburg PA
CBHW051049030426
42339CB00006B/268